CRIEFF PRIMARY SCHOO

649

Toys and Games

Ruth Thomson

Franklin Watts
London • New York • Sydney • Toronto

Note for parents and teachers

The Changing Times series is soundly based on the requirements of the new History Curriculum. Using the device of four generations of a real family, the author combines reminiscences of this family with other people's oral evidence. The oral history is matched with photographs and other contemporary sources. Many other lessons are hidden in the text, which practises the skills of chronological sequencing, gives reference to a timeline and introduces the language and vocabulary of the past. Young children will find much useful information here, as well as a new understanding of the recent history of everyday situations and familiar things.

© 1992 Franklin Watts

Franklin Watts
96 Leonard Street
London
EC2A 4RH

Franklin Watts Australia
14 Mars Road
Lane Cove
NSW 2066

UK ISBN: 0 7496 0873 0

10 9 8 7 6 5 4 3 2 1

Editor: Sarah Ridley
Designer: Sally Boothroyd
Educational consultant: John West
Picture researcher: Juliet Duff
Photographer: Peter Millard

Acknowledgements: The publishers would like to thank the following people and organisations for their help with the preparation of this book: Kevin McGimpsey, Chester Toy Museum; Helen Bliss-Williams, Baden and Margaret Pearce, Alice, Celia and Billy Perry, Chloë and Leo Thomson, Joanna, Ben and Sam Caird, Jessie Ridley and Jessie Baker for the loan of their toys, games and books.

A CIP catalogue record for this book is available from the British Library.

Printed in Malaysia

Contents

These are some of the toys
my friends and I play with.

For Christmas, I'm going to ask
for either a Game Boy
or a remote-controlled car.

My friend next-door likes playing with her Sylvanian families.

I like playing with Lego best of all.

My brother would like an electric train set.

After school, we watch
television or videos.

At weekends, we often go
to the park and ride our bikes.
Sometimes I play football.

Other children play
on roller skates
and skateboards.

We play on the swings
and slides.

I asked Dad if he played with the same toys and games when he was young.

Dad said,

'I spent most of my time playing with metal model cars. There weren't many plastic ones.'

'I had a Meccano set. I made all sorts of models with it.'

'My little brother liked playing with robots and space figures.'

8

'He was mad about
the Wild West.
He was always dressing up
as a cowboy.'

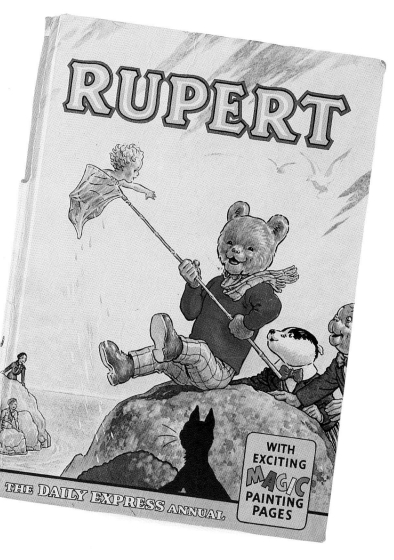

'We all read comics
and annuals.
My favourite was *Rupert*.
I was given an annual
every Christmas.'

Mum said,

'I had a Barbie doll.
Barbie was a new toy then.
Every girl I knew
either had one or wanted one.'

'We played a lot
of indoor games
or did jigsaws.'

'My sister and I spent hours setting out our farm animals and making up stories about them.'

'I loved pogoing.'

'I took my teddy to bed with me until I was almost a teenager.'

I asked Grandad what he played with when he was my age.

He said,

'I played with lots of model cars.'

'I had a clockwork train. It went round and round on an oval track.'

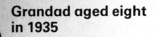

'My Meccano set
was my pride and joy.'

'I played cricket
in the street
with my friends.'

I asked Granny what she played with when she was a child.

She said,

'We played a lot outside.'

'We had a big craze for cigarette cards. We flicked them against a wall. If you got one card on top of another, you won it.'

'At home, I spent ages cutting out paper doll's clothes or arranging my farm animals.'

'Every week, we got a comic. I read it first, because I was the eldest.'

Grandad said,

'At Christmas, the whole family played all sorts of indoor games.'

Draughts

Blow football

Happy families

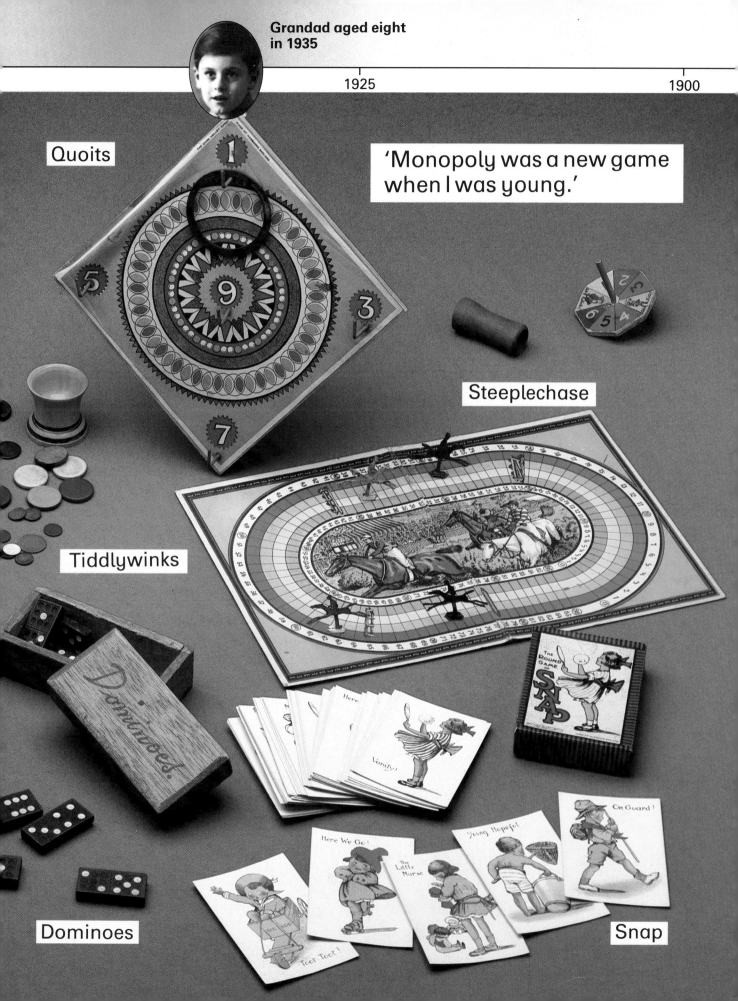

Grandad aged eight in 1935

1925

1900

Quoits

'Monopoly was a new game when I was young.'

Steeplechase

Tiddlywinks

Dominoes

Snap

When Grandad was growing up, the war started against Germany.

He said,

'Children bought more toy guns, lead soldiers and dressing up clothes.'

Lead soldiers

'We played pretend war games. I was a soldier and my sister was a nurse.'

'As the war went on, you couldn't buy toys in the shops any more. The toy factories made tanks instead.'

18

'I collected
war souvenirs –
planes and badges,
and bits of bombs.'

'I had a spotter book
of aeroplanes.
I knew them all.'

Spot them in the Air!

3^D

PUBLISHED BY THE
DAILY MIRROR

'London children played games
on bomb sites.'

I asked Great-granny what sort of toys
she had when she was a child.

She said,

'There weren't so many toys
in my day and we had to help
our parents more.'

'We had to make our own fun.
Most of our games cost nothing.
There wasn't much room
to play inside in our house.
We played in the street.'

'There was a lot of sitting on doorsteps. We talked, joked and played games.'

'On Sundays, we'd skip in the street. You couldn't do that on weekdays. It was too busy with horses and vans.'

Great-granny said,

'If you were lucky,
you had a scooter.
They were great fun.
I never had one of my own.'

'The boys played marbles
in the gutter.'

'The big prize ones
were called *glarneys.*'

'The boys made carts
out of a piece of wood.
They fixed a box
on top and pram wheels
underneath.'

23

Great-granny said,

'Some children had wooden hoops, which they rolled along with a stick.'

'I had a wooden top. The whip was a piece of Dad's bootlace.'

'My most precious toy
was a doll.
She had a china head,
which I chose,
and a rag body.'

'I always wanted a tricycle.
My cousin had one.
Sometimes she let me have a go.'

25

'We loved looking in toyshop windows, but we never dared go inside.'

'I loved books. My aunt gave me one every Christmas.'

'I always wanted a Noah's Ark
with all those pairs of animals.'

Things to do

Look at these toys. What are they made of?

Nintendo game

Troll

Clockwork bike

Picture blocks

Ask your parents and grandparents
what sort of toys they had.
Were they made of wood, plastic, metal, rubber or cloth?

Metal aeroplane

How did their toys work –
by clockwork or by battery?

Plastic space figure

Alphabet tray

Which toys do you think your parents played with?
Which ones do you see now?

Find out what sort of construction toys
grown-ups had when they were young.
Show them these pictures to help remind them.

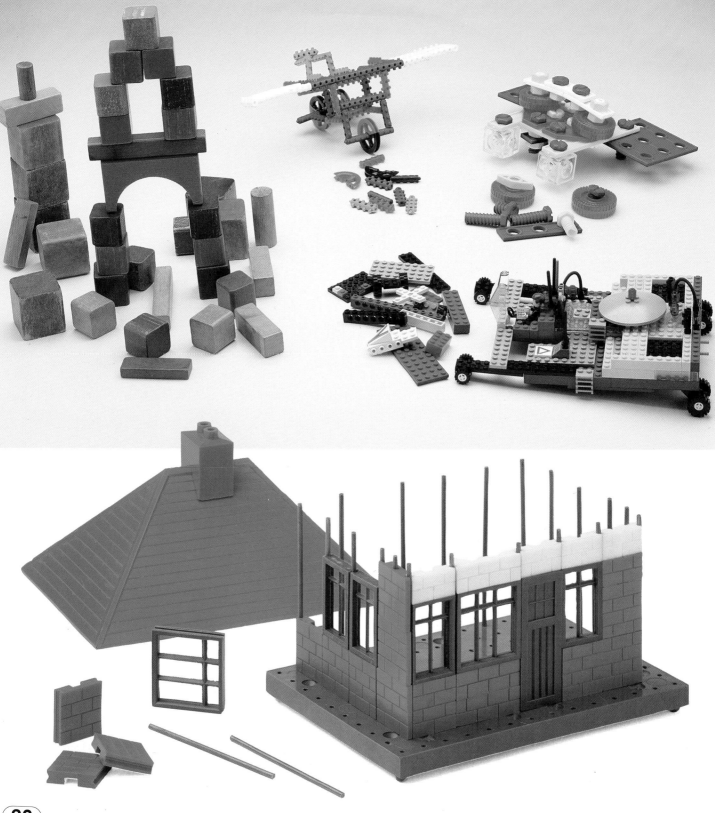

Have you seen dolls like these?
Which one do you think
is the oldest and which is the newest?

Ask your family which ones they remember
from when they were young.

Index

Photographs: Beamish endpapers, 21(t), 22(t); © Britt Allcroft (Thomas) Limited 1992 5(b); Mary Evans Picture Library 25(tr); Eye Ubiquitous 6(b); Chris Fairclough 4(b); Chris Fairclough Colour Library 7(t); Francis Frith Collection title page (t), 25(bl); Sally and Richard Greenhill 6(c), 7(bl), 7(br); Hulton Picture Company cover (tl), cover (br), 11(bl), 13(b), 23(b), 24(t); Lego UK Ltd title page (b); Matchbox Toys Ltd cover (br); Peter Millard imprint page, 4(t), 5(c), 6(tr), 8(t), 9(r), 10(l), 11(t), 11(br), 15(bl), 16-17, 18(tr), 22(bl), 24(b), 26(b), 27, 28, 29, 30, 31; Museum of Childhood, Edinburgh/Forth Photography 15(br); Nick Nicholson 8(b), 12(t); thanks to Nintendo Game Boy 28(tl); Stephen Oliver 5(t), 10(r), 15(t); Robert Opie 12(b), 13(t), 19(tr), 23(t); Popperfoto 14; Nicholas Ridley 18(bl); Topham cover (tr), 20, 21(b), 26(t).

Hearing sounds can keep us safe, too. A horn on a car can warn us to stay on the pavement. A smoke alarm in a building can warn us of danger. We hear sounds because they travel from their **sources** (the things that made them) to our ears.

Be a sound detective

Find a good place to sit, such as a park or in a window looking over a street. Write down what sounds you hear. Then try to write down what made the sounds, especially when you cannot see the source!

When set off, a smoke alarm is loud and constant, so no one can ignore it!

How sound moves to our ears

Things that make sound **vibrate**. They move up and down or backwards and forwards very quickly. If you wrap an elastic band around your fingers and pluck it, you will see and feel it vibrate. As an object vibrates, it bumps into the air around it. When this air vibrates, it bumps into the air next to it. This keeps happening until the air **vibrations** reach our ears and we hear the sounds.

Drawing a bow across violin strings makes them vibrate. These vibrations create the sounds of music.

Have you ever thrown a pebble into a pond or the sea? Little waves ripple out in circles from the place where the pebble splashed into the water. The way these little waves move across the water is similar to how sound vibrations spread out through the air. That is why they are called **sound waves**.

Sound travels in waves from the **source** of the sound to our ears.

Sound signals

Sound waves spread out and travel in all directions. That is how sounds warn us of dangers we cannot see behind us, such as a speeding car or an angry dog!

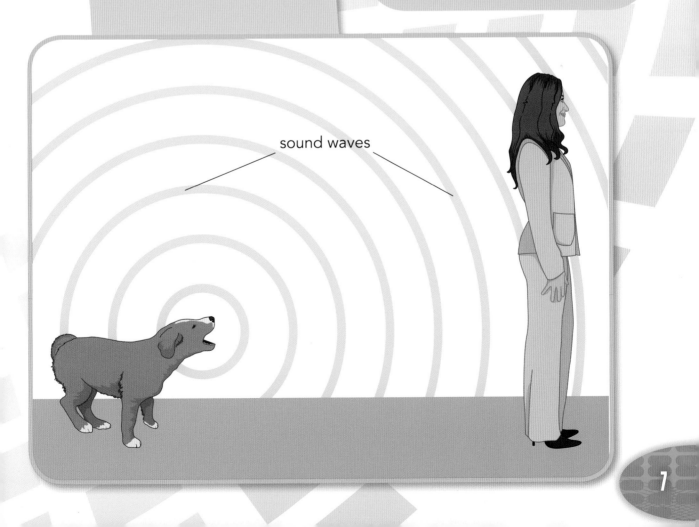

sound waves

Activity: Testing ears

Why do we have two ears? What do you think will happen when we hear sounds with one ear instead of two? Try this test to find out.

What you need

- Blindfold
- Six friends

What to do

 1 Ask one friend to sit in the middle of the room and put a blindfold on them.

 2 Ask the rest to stand about 3 metres (10 feet) away from them in a circle.

3 The person wearing the blindfold covers one ear. Then the people in the circle take turns to clap softly. Can the person wearing the blindfold point to exactly where the sound is coming from?

4 Do the clapping test again, but this time the person wearing the blindfold should uncover both ears.

5 Repeat the test for different people wearing the blindfold. This makes it a fair test because some people hear better than others.

What happens?

Most people point in the right direction when they use both ears. It is easier to judge distance using two ears because the ear closest to the sound hears it a little louder and slightly sooner than the other ear.

Hearing through things

Sounds usually travel through the air to our ears, but sound can move through other **materials**, too. Sound can travel through **solids**, such as metal and wood. It can also travel through **liquids**, such as water. That is why you can hear someone knocking on a wooden door or calling you when your head is under water in the bath or pool!

Sound travels better through some materials than others. Sound vibrations travel well through wood.

Sound waves need a material to travel through to reach our ears so we can hear them. Between the stars and planets in space, there is nothing. There is no air. When something **vibrates**, there is nothing for it to bump into, so it cannot pass on those **vibrations**. That means sound waves cannot travel in space, so it is totally silent!

Outside a spacecraft, astronauts talk to each other through radios in their helmets.

Air in space

When people travel in space, their spacecraft contains air for them to breathe. This also means astronauts can talk normally. Outside the spacecraft, there is no sound.

Activity: Sounds through solids

Do you think sounds travel better through a **solid**, such as wood, than a **gas**, such as air? Try this activity to see if you are right.

What you need

- Desk
- Pin
- One friend

What to do

1 Sit at a desk, either facing away from your friend or with your eyes closed. Ask your friend to drop the pin on the desk. Make sure your friend is careful of the sharp end and that they do not drop the pin too near you. Did you hear it drop? How loud was the sound?

1

2 Now rest your head flat on the desk. Ask your friend to drop the pin on the desk, again so you cannot see it drop. Is the sound different when your ear is on the desk and you hear it through the wood?

2

Find out more

You could try the same test on a metal surface to find out if sound vibrations travel better through metals than wood.

What happens?

You should discover that the sound of the pin dropping on the desk is louder or easier to hear through wood. In fact, **sound waves** travel around 13 times faster in wood than air. That is because even tiny **vibrations**, such as those made by a pin dropping, travel faster through solids than through a gas.

How do our ears work?

We don't just use our ears to hear sounds. We use our brain, too! Did you know that the ear flaps you can see on the outside of your head are only a small part of your ears? The most important parts of the ear are actually inside the head. The ear flaps do have an important job to do. They collect **sound waves** and send them into the ear along a short tunnel called the **ear canal**.

The shape of the outer ear helps it to collect sounds. If you cup your hand around your ear, you will see how this works.

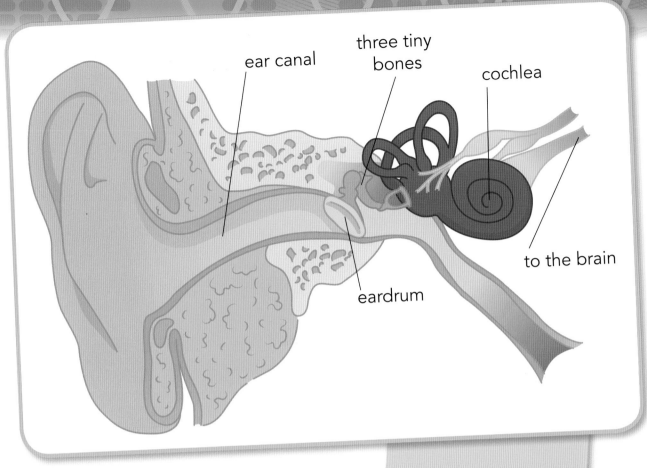

ear canal

three tiny bones

cochlea

to the brain

eardrum

This picture shows the different parts inside the ear.

At the end of the ear canal there is a thin piece of skin called the **eardrum**. The eardrum is stretched tight, like a drum. When sound waves hit it, the eardrum **vibrates** and passes these vibrations along three tiny bones. These tiny bones pass the **vibrations** into the **cochlea**. The cochlea is full of **liquid**. The vibrations create tiny waves in the liquid that help to change the sound waves into signals that go to the brain. Then the brain works out what the sounds are!

Activity: Make an eardrum

Make a model to test what happens to the **eardrum** when **sound waves** hit it.

What you need
- Metal bowl
- Cling film
- Large elastic band
- Uncooked rice
- Saucepan
- Wooden spoon

What to do

1 Stretch a sheet of cling film over the bowl. Make sure the cling film is tight and smooth. Put the elastic band around the cling film to make sure it stays on tightly. This is your eardrum!

2 Sprinkle some rice over the surface of the stretched cling film.

3 What do you think will happen if you hold the saucepan near the drum and hit the saucepan with the spoon to make a loud sound?

4 Try it. Were you right?

4

What happens?

You should see the rice bouncing on the cling film. **Vibrations** from the **source** of the sound made the air **vibrate** and that made the cling film and then the rice move. Like the cling film eardrum, your real eardrum vibrates in time to the sound waves that enter the ear.

Try this!

Do you think the rice will move less or more when you hit the pan softer and harder to make quieter and louder sounds? Try it.

Animal hearing

Animals use their ears to hear danger or to listen for smaller animals to catch and eat. Many animals hear like us, but have different shaped ears. Some animals have very large ears to help them collect **sound waves**. Some have ears that can move and point in different directions to collect sound better.

Ears on legs?

Some animals have ears in places other than their heads. A cricket picks up sound waves when they **vibrate** a thin skin called a **membrane** on its front legs!

A kangaroo can twist both of its huge ears in different directions to listen out for danger.

Dolphins are able to hear 14 times better than humans!

Dolphins and some whales use clicks and whistles to talk. Other whales produce sound (and breathe) through the blowholes on the top of their heads. The sound **vibrations** they make can travel a long way in the oceans. That is because sound travels five times faster and further in water than it does in air.

Underwater hearing

Humans do not hear so clearly under water because when our ears fill up with water, the **eardrums** cannot vibrate as well. In dolphins, sound waves get to the inner ear through the bones of its mouth!

Activity: Water and sounds

Test how well **sound waves** can travel under water.

What you need
- Empty, clean 2-litre (4-pint) plastic bottle
- Scissors
- Sink or large plastic tub
- Water
- Two stones

What to do

1 Ask an adult to help you cut off the bottom of the plastic bottle.

2 Fill your sink with water, but not to the top. Hold the plastic bottle in the water so that the bottom half is under the water, but not touching the sink, and the top half is out of the water.

3 Put your ear to the top of the bottle. Ask your friend to bang the two stones together under the water.

3

4 Now lift the bottle out of the water and put your ear to the top of the bottle again. Listen to your friend banging the stones together in the air. The stones should be the same distance away from the bottle as they were under water to make this a fair test. Did you hear the sound better through the air or the water?

4

What happens?

Sound **vibrations** travel faster through water than through air. The sound of the stones banging together should be louder when you listen to it with the bottle under water.

Helping us to hear things

Some machines help us to hear things. Inside a **microphone** there is a thin **membrane** that **vibrates** when **sound waves** hit it. This makes a coil of wire vibrate. As the coil of wire moves, it turns the **vibrations** into electric signals. **Electricity** is a sort of **energy** that can be changed into other types of energy. The electricity signals flow through wires to a **loudspeaker**. The loudspeaker changes the signals back into sound waves and makes the sounds louder.

Microphones change sounds into a form of electricity so the sounds can be recorded or played back louder through a loudspeaker.

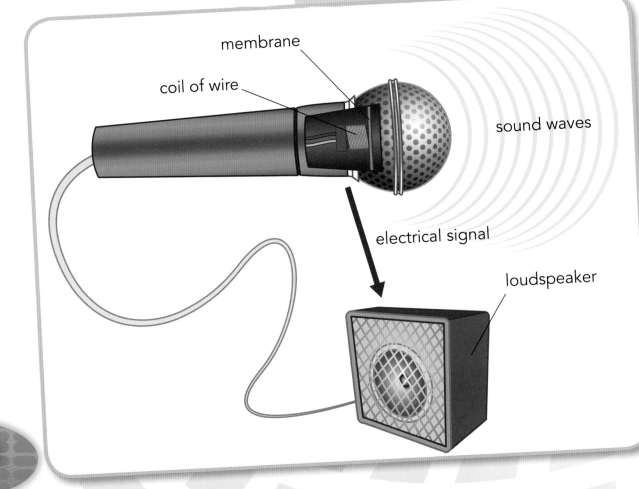

membrane

coil of wire

sound waves

electrical signal

loudspeaker

We can use telephones to talk to people a long way away.

Landline telephones have a microphone in their mouthpiece. These change sound waves from our voice into electric signals. These signals travel through wires until they get to the telephone of the person we are calling. A small loudspeaker in this telephone changes the signals back into sound waves so friends can hear what we are saying.

Mobile phones

Mobile phones do not need wires. Microphones in mobile phones turn sound waves into a type of energy called **radio waves**. These carry signals through the air.

Activity: A string telephone

Make your own simple telephone.

What you need
- Two plastic cups
- Sharp pencil
- String (kite string or fishing line work well)
- Two paper clips
- One friend

What to do

1 Cut a piece of string, about 10 metres (33 feet) long.

2 Ask an adult to use the pencil to make a small hole in the bottom of each cup. Push one end of the string through each cup. Tie the ends to paper clips to stop them coming out.

3 You and your friend each take a cup and move apart until the string is stretched out. Make sure the string is tight and not touching anything. Why do you think this is important?

4 Hold the cup to your ear and listen while your friend whispers into their cup. Then swap, so you whisper into your cup while your friend listens. What can you both hear?

What happens?

When you talk into the plastic cup, the air in the cup **vibrates**. The **vibrations** go along the string to the other cup and make air in the other cup vibrate. Sound travels better through **solids** than air, so the listener can hear what the other says even when they talk very quietly. (If the string is too loose, the vibrations will not be carried.)

When ears do not work

Some people cannot hear as well as others. People who cannot hear well often wear a hearing aid. This picks up sounds from outside and makes them louder so the wearer can hear better. Some people are born with hearing problems or get them as a result of an illness. Some children get a problem called glue ear that makes it harder to hear, but it usually clears up quickly by itself.

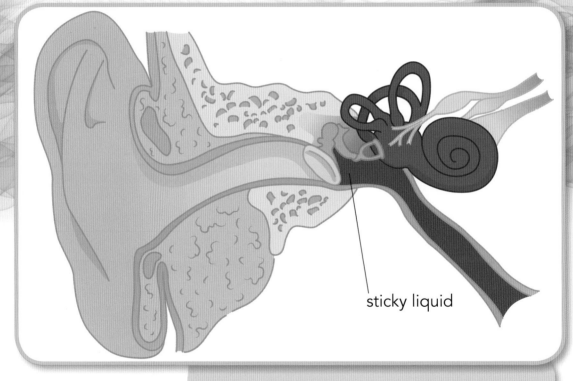

sticky liquid

With glue ear, a sticky **liquid** fills the space behind the eardrum. This stops the tiny bones in the ear moving properly, so they cannot pass on sound vibrations to the **cochlea** so well.

Ear safety

You can damage ears by listening to very loud sounds. So do not turn the **volume** on your earphones up too high. Do not poke things in your ears as this could hurt your **eardrum**.

People who are deaf cannot hear any sounds. They rely on their other **senses** to help them. Many people who are deaf still play and enjoy music. Instead of hearing the sounds with their ears, they feel the **vibrations** through other parts of their body.

Some deaf musicians play barefoot so they can feel the vibrations from the floor through their feet.

Sign language

Many people who are deaf learn to use sign language. Sign language uses hand signals instead of speaking. Thousands of deaf and hearing people use sign language.

There are signs for each letter in the alphabet. There are also signs for words and phrases.

Deaf or hard-of-hearing students can talk to their teacher using sign language.

Here a speech is being translated into sign language for the deaf or hard-of-hearing people in the audience.

Differences

Just as different countries speak different languages, they also use different sign languages. The United Kingdom uses British Sign Language (BSL) and the United States uses American Sign Language (ASL). Find out more on page 31.

Glossary

cochlea tube in the ear shaped like a snail's shell that sends sound messages to the brain

ear canal short tunnel that goes from the ear flap into the main part of the ear

eardrum thin piece of skin at the end of the ear canal that vibrates like a drum when sound waves hit it

electricity type of energy we usually use to make machines work

energy power that makes things work or move

gas thing that has no shape or size of its own. Gases, such as the air in the sky, can spread out in all directions and change shape to fill any space.

liquid thing that is runny and cannot be held easily in your hands, such as water, milk, or juice

loudspeaker machine that changes electric signals into sound waves and releases them into the air

material something we use or make other things from, such as wood, rubber, or plastic

membrane very thin layer of material, such as skin or plastic

microphone machine that picks up sounds and changes them into signals that can be carried along electrical wires

radio wave type of energy that can carry sounds and pictures through the air, often over long distances

sense one of the five powers (sight, hearing, smell, taste, and touch) that your body uses to get information about the world around it

solid thing that has a definite shape and always takes up the same amount of space. Many solids are hard, such as wood or metal.

sound wave vibration in the air that we hear as sound

source person or thing that starts something

vibrate, vibration move forwards and backwards or up and down very quickly, again and again

volume loudness of a sound

Find out more

Books

Adventures in Sound (Graphic Science), Emily Sohn (Raintree, 2010)

Ear-splitting Sounds and Other Vile Noises (Disgusting & Dreadful Science), Anna Claybourne (Franklin Watts, 2013)

Sound (The Science Detective Investigates), Harriet McGregor (Wayland, 2011)

Websites

www.britishsignlanguage.com/words/list.php

You can learn lots more words and phrases in sign language on this website.

www.childrensuniversity.manchester.ac.uk/interactives/science/brainandsenses/ear

www.kidshealth.org/kid/htbw/ears.html

You can find out more about how your ears work on these websites.

www.dangerousdecibels.org/virtualexhibit/2howdowehear.html

You can find out about loud sounds and how they hurt ears on this website.